Inventions That CHANGED the WORLD

How the Internet Changed the World

Kaitlyn Duling

Cavendish Square
New York

Published in 2019 by Cavendish Square Publishing, LLC
243 5th Avenue, Suite 136, New York, NY 10016

First Edition

Library of Congress Cataloging-in-Publication Data

Names: Duling, Kaitlyn, author.
Title: How the Internet changed the world / Kaitlyn Duling.
Description: First edition. | New York : Cavendish Square Publishing, LLC, 2019. | Series: Inventions that changed the world | Includes bibliographical references and index. | Audience: Grades 5 to 8.
Identifiers: LCCN 2018021942 (print) | LCCN 2018022336 (ebook) | ISBN 9781502641120 (ebook) | ISBN 9781502641113 (library bound) | ISBN 9781502641106 (pbk.)
Subjects: LCSH: Internet--History--Juvenile literature. | Internet--Social aspects--Juvenile literature.
Classification: LCC TK5105.875.I57 (ebook) | LCC TK5105.875. I57 D85 2019 (print) | DDC 303.48/33--dc23
LC record available at https://lccn.loc.gov/2018021942

Editorial Director: David McNamara
Editor: Kristen Susienka
Copy Editor: Alex Tessman
Associate Art Director: Alan Sliwinski
Designer: Joe Parenteau
Production Coordinator: Karol Szymczuk
Photo Research: J8 Media

The photographs in this book are used by permission and through the courtesy of: Cover Busakorn Pongparnit/Getty Images; p. 4 Shutterstock.com; p. 6 Denys Prykhodov/Shutterstock.com; p. 7 Fat Camera/Shutterstock.com; p. 8 Daniel M Ernst/Shutterstock.com; p. 11 hutch photography/Shutterstock.com; p. 12 AP Images; p. 15 U.S. Army Photo/ Wikimedia Commons/File:Eniac.jpg/Public Domain; p. 17 ARPANET/Wikimedia Commons/File:Arpanet map 1973.jpg/ Public Domain; p. 20 Fabrice Coffrini/AFP/Getty Images; p. 23 Philippe DesMazes/AFP/Getty Images; p. 27 Evannovostro/ Shutterstock.com; p. 28 Goodluz/Shutterstock.com; p. 30 Monkey Business Images/Shutterstock.com; p. 33 Raybon009/ iStockphoto.com; p. 35 Tero Vesalainen/Shutterstock.com; p. 38 Antoniodiaz/Shutterstock.com; p. 40 MNStudio/ Shutterstock.com; p. 42 Visual China Group/Getty Images; p. 44 Raysonho@Open Grid Schedule/ Grid Engine/ Wikimedia Commons/File:Nest Learning Thermostat (cropped).JPG/Public Domain; p. 47 Alexsi/iStockphoto.com; p. 48 Redpixel.PL/Shutterstock.com; p. 52 Yacobchuk/iStock/Thinkstock; p. 54 Rawpixel.com/Shutterstock.com.

Printed in the United States of America

CONTENTS

ONE Getting Connected 5

TWO Inventing the Internet 13

THREE Life Online 29

FOUR The Internet Today and Tomorrow 45

Glossary 55

Further Information 58

Selected Bibliography 60

Index 62

About the Author 64

We connect to the internet in numerous ways—through computers, smartphones, tablets, televisions, and more!

CHAPTER ONE

Getting Connected

When you think of the internet, you might picture a computer, a tablet, or a smartphone. You may think of browsing web pages, sending email, and playing games online. However, the internet is much more than that. In fact, it is woven through almost every moment of our daily lives. There are very few things we do that are not touched by this amazing invention.

Yes, the internet was invented! It didn't just appear out of thin air or occur suddenly in nature. Twentieth-century humans created this tech tool that is now such a constant part of our existence. It is the bedrock of many modern communities. These days, it is often considered a necessary part of life.

A Day in the (Connected) Life

The internet is accessible at any time, day or night. Within the first moments of our waking, we have access to the internet. We can unlock our phone screens and press a button that connects us instantly. During the night, we can keep our homes at comfy temperatures using internet-connected thermostats. At breakfast, you might scroll social media apps on your phone or read on a tablet that is connected to Wi-Fi. Your refrigerator, television, and even your bathroom scale could be connected to the internet. If you miss the school bus, you can look up a number for an Uber. With the internet, no one has to worry about being late. Those who drive or use public transportation can use GPS applications that will say the quickest route out loud.

These days, many cars offer access to data, Wi-Fi, and Bluetooth technologies. You can talk on the phone, use GPS, and stream music, all from the driver's seat.

The internet has become a vital part of education. Computers, tablets, and Smartboards are all common features in both public and private schools and colleges.

At school, there are many internet-connected tech tools. Teachers have desktop computers with web-based grade books. Classrooms have "smart" boards and projectors. Tablets and laptops are used during class. When a film is shown in class, it will most likely be downloaded from the internet. And research? In addition to books, we access articles from online databases.

During relaxation time, we don't escape the internet. Whether it's streaming video, browsing websites, shopping online, sending pictures to friends, or making plans using online schedules, the internet is everywhere. Today, you can be connected in your home, school, workplace, and even in your vehicle. Trains and airplanes have Wi-Fi too! When you need to do tasks like order takeout, check sports scores, make an appointment for a haircut, or submit homework, you may do so online. The internet has revolutionized the way we communicate, work, travel, and live.

Going Without

You might ask yourself if you could survive without the internet. Yes, you could. In fact, many people around the world live in countries that are not saturated with the internet and data. There are still places where students do not go online for homework help, where videos do not stream on tablets, and where wedding invitations are sent by postal mail rather than email. However, modern life in the United States, Canada, and other technologically advanced countries is built for an internet-connected society. Checking for up-to-date weather reports, using

Without the internet, people are forced to talk! Phone calls, letters, and face-to-face conversations are all communication tools that remain available, even if some have gone out of style.

SOCIAL MEDIA

One of the most popular uses of the internet today is communication on social media. Facebook, Twitter, Instagram, Snapchat, LinkedIn, and others are all forms of social media. They are considered "social" forms of media because they help people share information. You might share pictures, words, ideas, jokes, or news. Through social media, people can communicate twenty-four hours a day, seven days a week. Information can be shared immediately, without waiting.

Before social media, email and instant messaging dominated the internet. People could use these tools to send messages between themselves and other people. However, today, social media allows us to connect with more people faster. It even helps us connect with celebrities and strangers. Brands use social media to promote their products. Do you use social media? How does it make you feel? Researchers are still learning about its effects on our health and well-being.

a digital map, renewing library books, and other tasks sometimes *require* the use of the internet. Other tasks, like buying concert tickets, making dinner reservations, and connecting with old friends, are simply easier to do with the help of the internet. If you find yourself wanting to quit the internet—try it! It may be easier or harder than you first expect.

Some communities in the United States, such as the Amish, choose not to interact with the internet. They rely on face-to-face communication, the US Postal Service, public libraries, and other tools. These help them live without the convenience of the World Wide Web. A lack of internet connectivity changes everything. Without online shopping, people must physically travel to stores. In order to talk to someone, people are forced to visit in-person or talk on the phone. Books, mail, social skills, meetings, and other things gain importance. Without time spent browsing websites, scrolling through Facebook, checking the current weather, and reading up-to-the-minute sports updates, time is freed for other activities. More time can be spent outside. More in-person conversations can occur. Life looks very different!

DID YOU KNOW:

Before email, many people communicated via telegraph. Invented in the mid-1800s, the telegraph transmitted messages on wires laid between locations. It used a code made of dots and dashes to express ideas without an alphabet.

In Amish communities, technology is avoided. This family doesn't use the internet, wear modern clothes, or drive a car. Instead, they get around by horse-drawn buggy.

These are some positive side effects of a lack of internet, but if connectivity suddenly disappeared on a large scale, much of the world would come to a halt. Banks, businesses, libraries, news outlets, and other places rely heavily on the internet. Even energy suppliers and transportation companies, like airlines, are dependent on the internet. The GPS apps we all use to get directions and the iPad payment system at your favorite café also rely on it. Without the internet, these services would be nearly impossible to operate as effectively as they are now.

For better or worse, we live in a connected society. It's up to us to learn about how we got here, what it means for us as a worldwide community, and the ways in which we should continue to connect (or not) as we move forward and make progress.

Netscape Navigator was one of the first internet browsers, released in 1994. Netscape browsers remained popular throughout the 1990s. However, Netscape was eventually overshadowed by Internet Explorer and other browsers.

CHAPTER TWO

Inventing the Internet

Today, we use the internet as a communication tool. We use it for other things, of course—solving complex equations, organizing information, and storing media. However, we often use it to speak to one another through words, photos, videos, and more. We use social media. We read websites full of facts compiled by others. The internet helps us share information and learn together. It is an invaluable resource.

By the time the internet was invented in the twentieth century, humans had been communicating for thousands of years. First using speech, and then cave paintings and basic writing. The first postal service can be traced back to China in the year 900 BCE. It was used for communication between government officials. Throughout the next few hundred years, Grecians would use pigeons to send messages, clay moveable type would be invented in China, and then newspapers would appear in Europe around 1450. These were the first ways in which humans communicated with one another on a large scale.

After those first two thousand years, innovation sped up. The 1800s gave us the first photographs, telegraph, telephone, and movies. The first half of the twentieth century saw the introduction of radio, color printing, paperback books, television, and records. Now we could share information across communities, and even across the world. Just a few short decades later, computers were invented.

The First Computers

Originally, computers were like giant calculators. In fact, during the late 1940s and early 1950s, when computers were first invented, they were called "computing machines." These were complicated devices that "read" and stored information. Today, the ENIAC is widely known as the first electronic digital computer to be built in the United States.

The ENIAC couldn't be used to play games or read blogs. Its main function was to calculate tables used in aiming artillery, or weapons. It was kept secret for a while, until its identity was introduced to the public in 1946.

Computing machines like ENIAC looked nothing like the computers, laptops, and tablets we use today. In fact, they were so big they filled entire rooms. They were full of switches, plugs, and buttons that had to be manipulated in order to work the computer. Personal

These two workers are shown programming the ENIAC in Philadelphia, Pennsylvania.

computers (or PCs) didn't come around until decades later. The very first models were sold as kits that you had to put together yourself. These were introduced in 1975.

Throughout the 1970s and 1980s, personal computers grew more useful, and much smaller. Instead of just clunky, fancy typewriters, they could be used to play games and conduct business through spreadsheets and other software. Microsoft Word, which you might use for writing essays and speeches, was launched in 1983. By industry estimates, there were about one million personal computers in the United States by 1980. However, most of these were expensive. Not everyone had access to the new technology.

Dreaming Up the Internet

The 1980s and the rise of PCs paved the way for the birth of the internet. However, unlike the telephone or fidget spinner, the internet wasn't invented by just one or two people. It wasn't imagined and created within a matter of weeks or even years. The first rumblings about the very basic ideas behind the internet began in the 1960s. In August 1962, a man named Joseph Carl Robnett Licklider, a researcher at Massachusetts Institute of Technology (MIT), wrote a series of memos. These memos introduced the idea of a "network." A network is simply a system of things that are connected to each other. Licklider imagined a world in which computers were globally connected. Data and programs could be accessed from anywhere, at any time. Licklider was also head of the computer research program at the United States Department of Defense. He talked to his coworkers and convinced them that the idea of a network was one worth researching.

The research, funded by the Department of Defense, continued. During this time, Americans were thinking more seriously about science and technology. The government and civilians were concerned about the Cold War. This was a conflict brewing between the Soviet Union and the United States. The Soviets launched an impressive satellite in 1957, *Sputnik 1*. Advanced Soviet technology led schools, corporations, and governments in the United States to invest in scientific research. The Department of Defense hoped to develop new rockets, weapons, and technology that could be used to defend the country in times of war.

One project they funded was ARPANET. It stood for the Advanced Research Projects Agency Network. The experts at ARPANET formed the foundations of the network that would be used to create the internet. Up until the mid-1960s, most communication relied on circuit

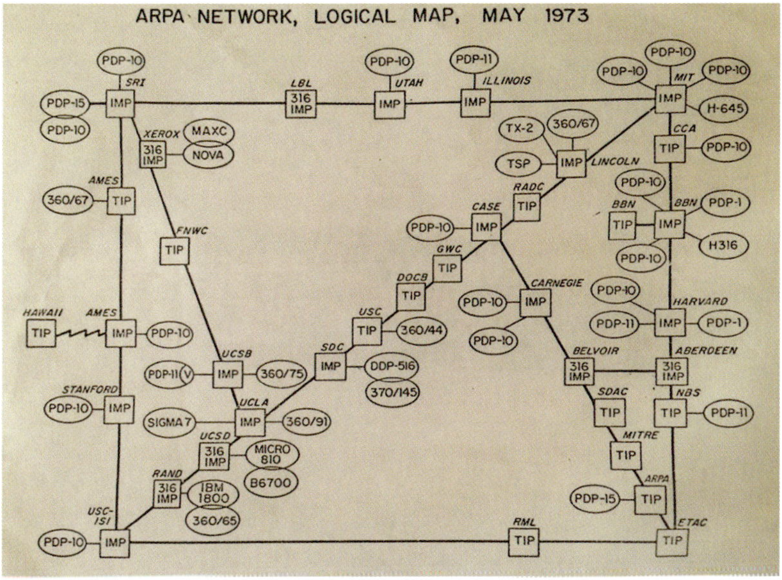

This 1973 map of ARPANET shows how the network reached from Hawaii and Stanford (*on the left*) to Harvard and MIT on the East Coast (*on the right*).

switching. This is the method used in a traditional landline telephone network. A telephone in Atlanta, Georgia, is temporarily connected to one in Chicago. The data (voices) communicate over the line. The link disappears when the call is over. At ARPANET, they formed a new method—packet switching. In this method, links can be developed between multiple pairs of receivers and transmitters. Information is broken down into "packets" that can travel on their own paths. For example, when you publish an article online, people all over the world can leave comments. You are all connected. This is the possibility that packet-switching represented.

At first, just two computers were connected via the ARPANET network. Computers at the University of

California Los Angeles and Stanford Research Institute were able to send a message between them without a physical connection such as a wire. They were simply sent over the network. Soon, "nodes," or branches, of the system were added in Utah and elsewhere in California. The number of connected computers grew to include many more. In October 1972, ARPANET was publicly demonstrated for the first time. It was during this time that an application was written for the network. This would allow users to send, receive, and file messages between nodes. It was called electronic mail, or email.

Of course, it wasn't just a free-for-all after email was invented. The network was still extremely small. It was not quite the internet we know today. It was still primarily funded by the US Department of Defense. A 1982 handbook on ARPANET use gave this warning about etiquette:

> *It is considered illegal to use the ARPANet for anything which is not in direct support of Government business ... personal messages to other ARPANet subscribers (for example, to arrange a get-together or check and say a friendly hello) are generally not considered harmful ... Sending electronic mail over the ARPANet for commercial profit or political purposes is both anti-social and illegal. By sending such messages, you can offend many people, and it is possible to get MIT in serious trouble with the Government agencies which manage the ARPANet.*

Today, people in most countries have freedom of speech when it comes to the internet. It is considered a public arena, open for sharing. However, this wasn't always the case. On the ARPANET and other early forms of the internet, users had to be extra careful about what they said and did.

Creating the Internet

While ARPANET and other networks existed for sending information between computers, there was no system to connect these networks to each other. Researchers recognized this roadblock. Robert E. Kahn, who worked at the US Department of Defense, and Vincent Cerf from Stanford, decided to work together on the issue. In the late 1970s, they figured out how to connect the mini-networks together. The solution was called Transmission Control Protocol (TCP) and later the term Internet Protocol was added. Now it is known as TCP/IP. The method rules how data can be moved, shared, and received over the internet.

Now that TCP/IP existed, the Department of Defense funded even more research into it. The word "internet" was coined in 1974. It was a way to shorten the word "internetworking." It was around this time that "internet" was used to describe the large TCP/IP network of connected devices. By 1982, the Department of Defense had declared that TCP/IP was the standard for military computer networking.

At the same time, universities and organizations across the world began to adopt TCP/IP. The internet began to take hold, still in a research-focused format, in Europe and Australia. It was often set up within research universities. As the years went on, South Korea, Japan, and Singapore all set up their own networks.

It was also during this time that the digital divide began to take shape. While technological advancements were made in many countries, developing areas were shut out of the networks due to a lack of infrastructure and/or funding. Without heavily funded research universities, many countries were unable to create their own networks. A lack of internet connectivity in developing countries is a challenge that continues today.

It is important to remember that these early years of the internet were not intended for personal use. It was created primarily for the government. In fact, commercial use was forbidden. Can you imagine that? Today, the internet is highly commercialized. We shop online. We see advertisements. Businesses have their own websites and Instagram accounts. But in the 1980s, that was not the case. It was a challenging time of growth for the new technology. Many groups were started in an effort to organize the internet in some coherent manner. Discussions were had about commercial uses and

Today, the CERN lab, where Tim Berners-Lee was working when he invented the World Wide Web, is outfitted with the latest technologies and huge computer banks.

community uses. Though the internet's roots were in research, many people were interested in allowing the internet to include the global community. It would take many years for that dream to become a reality.

The World Wide Web

From its initial seeds of innovation in the 1960s to the growth and change period of the 1980s, the internet had advanced and evolved. In the early 1990s, that evolution would lead to the internet we know today.

For decades, the internet had been a way to send files back and forth between computers that operated within networks. In 1990, an English scientist named Tim Berners-Lee, who was working at the CERN lab in Switzerland, developed the World Wide Web. The World Wide Web is an information space. You access pages inside the space by typing in an address, such as www.google.com. Then you can read the information on that page and interact with its links, which might bring you to other information. Sometimes we just call this "the web." The World Wide Web was the first web browser computer program. A browser is simply an application that retrieves, moves, and presents information resources. Google Chrome, Safari, and Firefox are three common web browsers. Today when you open these applications on a computer, phone, or tablet, you have access to web pages and links.

The first browsers were extremely clunky. In 1992, researchers at the University of Illinois created a new browser. At first, it was called Mosaic, but later they changed the name to Netscape. This was the first user-friendly browser. Regular people would be able to use it, not just experienced scientists. There were words and pictures on the page. There were links you could click. There was even a scrollbar, a new invention that people could use to move up and down a page.

In the early 1990s, the internet wasn't experienced in the same ways it is today. Emails, chat rooms, and personal websites were the most popular ways to use it. Businesses used the internet for basic communication, data storage, and other tasks. However, that would soon change, in some very big ways.

Who's In Charge Here?

One of the biggest challenges faced by the early inventors and adopters of the internet was the question of governance: who was in charge of the internet? Because the idea of the internet developed out of various research initiatives, it never had one true, leading body. Today, this remains the case.

At first, it was grown and governed by the US government. The US Department of Defense was involved in much of its initial founding. Later, organization of domain names and IP addresses moved to the National Science Foundation, and then to ICANN, a nonprofit organization contracted by the US Department of Commerce. ICANN stands for Internet Corporation for Assigned Names and Numbers. It coordinates several databases related to the running of the internet. Around the world, there are many organizations dedicated to the open development and use of the internet. Put simply, it takes many groups to run

TIM BERNERS-LEE

Tim Berners-Lee, credited with inventing the World Wide Web, has had an exciting career path. Today, he directs the World Wide Web Consortium (W3C). This group sets some of the technical standards for the internet.

Before becoming one of the founders of the internet age, Berners-Lee grew up in London, England. He obtained a degree in physics and eventually landed a job at CERN in Switzerland. At CERN, he developed his interest in sharing text electronically, which led to his invention—the very first web server and browser. It would become widely known as the World Wide Web.

The world's first website address was info.cern.ch. Berners-Lee and his colleagues put it online in 1991. Through the newfound World Wide Web, people were now able to locate web pages through URLs (Uniform Resource Locators) and publish them using HTML (Hypertext Markup Language). Berners-Lee has said that if he didn't come up with the idea, someone else would have. But all we know for sure is that his invention is one of the most monumental and invaluable contributions to the internet as we know it today.

Timothy Berners-Lee speaks at a web conference in 2018.

the internet, especially if we want to keep it accessible for all people. Nonprofit, for-profit, and governmental organizations are involved. As the internet is accessed by the global community, it takes people around the world to make sure that it runs smoothly.

Commercialization and the Dot-Com Boom

Before 1995, the internet was a little sterile and growing slowly. It was still mostly in the hands of the federal government, Department of Defense, and research groups. The Federal Networking Council (FNC), working with other organizations, helped to coordinate the ways in which information was shared on the internet in its earliest years. On October 24, 1995, the FNC passed a landmark resolution. Their writing defined the term "internet." They agreed:

> *"Internet" refers to the global information system that—(i) is logically linked together by a globally unique address space based on the internet Protocol (IP) or its subsequent extensions/follow-ons; (ii) is able to support communications using the Transmission Control Protocol/Internet Protocol (TCP/IP) suite or its subsequent extensions/follow-ons, and/or other IP-compatible protocols; and (iii) provides, uses or makes accessible, either publicly or privately, high level services layered on the communications and related infrastructure described herein.*

This is a pretty messy definition to the regular reader and internet user, but it sums up what the internet is for—sharing, communicating, and accessing information, either publicly or privately.

It was around this time that demand from the commercial sector convinced the National Science Foundation (NSF) to finally lift restrictions on commercial use of the internet. The NSF had been the "backbone" of the internet. It had regulated website creation and more. After commercialization, the internet moved out from under the control of the federal government and into the private sector. From then on, you didn't need to go to the government in order to register your domain name (like google.com). Instead, you went to a private company, which could charge you to register the name. This concept is still in place today.

After the internet officially became commercial, it grew quickly. Hundreds of businesses wanted to take advantage of the new opportunities provided by the internet. Companies now had the freedom to create websites, post advertisements, and sell goods online that would be shipped directly to a person's home. From about 1995/1997 to 2001, financial investors poured money into these businesses. With the rise of PCs and an increase in their affordability for families, more and more homes had access to the internet. Web browsers improved and became more visually pleasing. Finally, it was fun to spend time on the internet! There were games, businesses, and shopping. Schools began to teach computer education courses that included instructions on typing and how to use the internet.

As more people got online and started to experience the internet, enthusiasm grew. More money was invested in "dot-com" companies. Some of these companies sold products, while others provided services, offered contests, or stored videos. They had names like "pets.com," "iWon," and "geocities." Their stock prices went up and up. People thought that all of these companies would be successful. Everyone wanted to invest in the internet, and the companies grew very big very fast. It felt like a "sure thing." However, it wasn't. Within just a couple years, many of the dot-com companies lost their value. Several had to file bankruptcy and shut their doors. Even though the internet was an exciting place for businesses, many of them had spent money and grown too fast. One by one, these websites shut down.

After the dot-com boom and bust, companies were more careful with their marketing and growth. Investors were cautious about how they spent their money. For a while, computer programmers had a difficult time finding jobs, and fewer people went to college for computer-related careers. But since then, the industry has grown. Today, with the rise of smartphones, tablets, and connected households, the internet is everywhere.

DID YOU KNOW:

The internet is in outer space! Astronauts on the International Space Station connect to the internet through satellites. They have computers that they use to email, tweet, and complete work.

Smartphones and tablets allow us to use phones indoors, outside, and everywhere around the world.

Today's Reality

The internet is woven into nearly everything we do, but it's hard to say if anyone imagined the reach it would have in today's world. Tim Berners-Lee, who created the World Wide Web, has based almost his entire career on the development of the internet. Berners-Lee was there for the first challenges—making the internet accessible, figuring out how to organize and govern it, and opening it up for commercial use. Today, he has been speaking out about the challenges that lie ahead. He has expressed concern about the spread of news stories that aren't factual and the lack of control over our personal data.

These problems didn't appear out of nowhere. They are results of the messy, complicated, and sometimes incredible ways the internet has grown over time. Though it took decades for the internet to become as big and powerful as it is today, it continues to expand. Each year, the internet allows us to do more, do things faster, and work smarter. Now it's up to us to decide what we want the internet to look like in the future.

Tablets are uniquely portable. This gives students the opportunity to work outside the classroom.

CHAPTER THREE

Life Online

The first researchers at the US Department of Defense had to work blindly, more or less. Nothing like this had ever been invented. Yes, different technologies had influenced society. Televisions, telephones, and electricity all had huge impacts on the way people communicated and lived their day-to-day lives. However, the internet changed the world in another way. It allowed people living on opposite sides of the globe to communicate instantly, twenty-four hours a day, seven days a week. It built platforms for social movements. It created new industries. And it caused many new and unique challenges. For better or for worse, from the 1990s on, the internet became a staple for much of modern society. It has continued to grow and evolve ever since.

E-Commerce

One of the biggest effects the internet has had on the world is the rise of e-commerce. E-commerce refers to online shopping. For most of modern history, people bought food, furniture, clothing, and other goods in physical stores. A person would walk, ride, or drive to a store and purchase the items they needed. Sometimes, people would go to auctions where they would offer prices for items in a group setting. Open-air markets were popular, as well as ordering items from a paper catalogue and paying through the mail. None of these shopping options have gone away, but the ability to shop online has drawn many people away from these experiences.

Today, shoppers are more likely to purchase items through the internet. Instead of driving from store to store, a person can go online and click from website to

The internet has radically changed how we shop. Today, consumers can receive products on the same day they order them.

website, reading reviews, checking competitors' prices, and finding the best deal on shipping. When you shop online, you don't have to speak to shopkeepers, walk around a store, or carry your items home. They arrive right on your doorstep. A study by TechCrunch, conducted in 2016, stated 79 percent of US consumers were shopping online. In 2000, this number was only 22 percent.

Many shoppers would probably note that online shopping is more convenient and often helps careful customers find better deals. However, there are some downsides. Online shopping causes people to stay out of malls and other stores. It also keeps them away from local businesses. In many small towns across the United States, Main Street has been known for its local shops. Recently, however, many have become ghost towns as small stores are forced to shut their doors. Unable to compete with large companies that sell items at lower prices, these tiny stores often must charge higher prices for their products. This dissuades shoppers and prices the local stores out of the shopping game.

In addition to putting the crunch on Main Street, online shopping can cause other issues. When someone shops online, they don't pay local taxes, and sometimes they might pay no tax at all. This tax revenue doesn't go into the local community, like road maintenance, libraries, and other services that benefit the public. Additionally, even though online shopping might seem more transparent, it can contain counterfeit, or fake, items, as well as goods that arrive at a person's home looking different from the picture they saw on Amazon or Etsy.

Without picking up an object, feeling its quality, or trying it on, much is left up to expectation. When a person's hopes are dashed, it can be difficult to make quick, easy, affordable returns or exchanges. Sometimes online customers think they're getting a deal when really they are being tricked or misled.

It's easy to get online and shop. There are countless websites where people can buy clothing, car parts, and even groceries. People can easily schedule and cancel services, like hair appointments. Even with its flaws, e-commerce has made life easier in many ways.

Social Impacts

In addition to shopping, people are now able to use the internet to do another favorite activity—talk. From its beginning, the internet revolutionized the way people communicate. Through email and chat, we can talk to friends, strangers, and family who live almost anywhere. Writing to friends is nearly instantaneous. In fact, these days, people don't even need to write words. They can send photos, videos, and emojis that are received instantly. There's no waiting for someone to pick up the phone on the other end or waiting for a letter to arrive in the mail.

All of this hyper-speed communication has had a huge impact on society. Not only has it increased the frequency with which we communicate with others, but it has changed the people with whom we communicate. Before the internet, people knew the addresses and phone numbers of their close friends. To contact others, they flipped through phone books. Today, it is easy to find someone online. You can connect with friends on Facebook or Instagram. It takes little more than a few clicks to find and contact almost anyone in the world, as long as you know some basic information about them.

This ease of connection can be considered a good thing, as it can make us more social and widen our social circles. However, it also arises the issue of privacy. Online, it is extremely difficult to keep a person's information private. In fact, some would argue that nothing is private when it comes to the internet. Any picture, sentence, Tweet, or address that is posted online is immediately vulnerable to discovery. A personal photo could be seen by the public, even when shared inside an app that claims to make pictures disappear after a time. Credit card numbers, bank accounts, and even social security numbers are vulnerable to identity theft when they are shared online. More and more, social media sites and

Websites and browsers often store sensitive personal information without the user's knowledge. When using the internet, we should be aware of privacy issues.

governmental groups are taking up the issue of privacy and examining it, trying to figure out how to keep our online information secure. It is not an easy task.

Social communities on the internet are not always guaranteed to be friendly. Cyberbullying is a problem unique to the internet age. Before the internet, bullying took place face-to-face or sometimes over the phone. People sometimes lied about their identities, but misinformation was easier to detect. The internet has made it easy for people to "hide behind the screen," and make anonymous, hurtful, and sometimes hateful comments—sometimes to people they've never met in person.

Cyberbullying can happen on both small and large scales. Students can gang up on another student online, spread lies about them, share photos, or simply be mean. Larger groups of people sometimes target certain people or groups. This is called trolling. In 2014, several female video game developers and bloggers were targeted in a trolling incident known as "Gamergate." Supporters of Gamergate anonymously worked together to harass and threaten the female gamers for months. This type of incident is not limited to Gamergate, however. It happens every day. Treatment like this could cause harmful depression in people of all ages.

The internet is one of the best covers a person has when they want to bully, harass, threaten, or target another human being. This is an issue that governments, law enforcement, courts, technology companies, and educators are all working on in their own ways. There is no simple solution.

Safety and Security

The internet is a wild and wonderful place. Since it does not exist in the physical world, there are none of the usual systems that protect us. Community helpers like the police, firefighters, and security guards are not present in the same way when we go online. When it comes to safety, we have had to figure out how to keep people safe online. Safety tactics have evolved over the years alongside the growth of the internet.

You might be thinking, "Online safety? Who needs that?" But with such an open and expansive network of individuals and groups, there's much that can go wrong. Not everyone on the internet can be trusted. People sell illegal goods, attack others, and steal information. Hacking is a huge problem. Hackers can steal and damage software,

Having strong passwords is one way to keep your information safe from potential online hackers.

information, and even identities. When a network or system is vulnerable, a hacker can sneak into the system through the internet, taking control of computers and personal information. They can lock a computer. They can shut down entire networks and businesses. They can spy on others. They can pretend to be someone else. They can steal passwords, credit card information, and usernames. They can spread misinformation. There's quite a lot that can go wrong online when we aren't attuned to cybersecurity. Those are the techniques we use to protect networks, programs, and data. Cybersecurity experts in the government, corporations, schools, and other places help protect people against attacks, damage, and unauthorized access.

Individuals can protect themselves online by following a few basic principles: never give out passwords, don't post personal information such as phone numbers or home addresses, think carefully about posting personal pictures or photos, keep privacy settings high, don't type something online that the person wouldn't say to someone's face, and don't befriend anyone who the person doesn't know in real life. These are simple steps that anyone can take.

If you're interested in cybersecurity as a career, look into it. As the internet grows and more people around the world get online, we will need more people to work in this field. Protecting governments, businesses, and everyday citizens from attack, and even from cyberterrorism, is an extremely important and necessary job.

THE POWER OF AN INTERNET MOVEMENT

Today, social movements don't just happen in public. Many of them are born on the internet and get much of their power from social media. Though many people march in the streets and speak out in public about certain ideas, they also have strong backing online, especially on Twitter and Facebook. Discussions about the issues happen there. Videos are posted. Photos are shared. People plan to protest.

Other movements depend on the internet for their structure. It Gets Better, the community of people speaking out on camera about how life gets better for LGBTQ individuals when they grow up, began on YouTube. Similarly, the #MeToo movement, centered on women's rights to personal safety, is based around a hashtag. The hashtag encouraged conversation, sharing stories, and speaking out. It would surely be much more difficult to harness so many voices, and the power of so many different people, without the use of the internet.

Medical Effects

Opportunities on the internet seem endless. Is there anything we *can't* do online? Some days, it may seem like the internet is the one-stop shop for everything we need in life. But researchers in the medical and child development fields are crying out—"Wait!" There's more to life than the internet! For all of the convenience, fun, and freedom it brings, too much internet can actually be harmful, in more ways than one.

Are we addicted to our phones? Some doctors and researchers think so. It's easy to imagine, especially since people seem to be on their phones all the time, even when hanging out with friends and family.

Even though the internet is still a relatively new invention, it has been known to cause mental and emotional problems for many people. "Technology addiction" is not listed in the latest version of the *Diagnostic and Statistical Manual of Mental Disorders*, the book that professionals use to diagnose psychiatric disorders. However, doctors know that internet addiction and gaming addiction are real issues. Furthermore, the internet can strengthen addictions that people already face, such as gambling or shopping, by making it easy to do those activities without leaving home.

Device screens and features, especially when connected to the internet or data, are built to be addictive. Games, apps, and even social media sites are created with addiction in mind. Developers want consumers to return again and again, to spend money and use their products. But becoming addicted can have negative effects in personal, familial, financial, and academic areas of life. Relationships can be harmed. School and jobs can be ignored. And, when they're in the deep throes of addiction and trying to escape, people can experience withdrawal symptoms, much like one would when quitting cigarettes or alcohol. Sadness, anger, anxiety, irritability, and even nausea can all be caused by withdrawal from an internet addiction. Of course, there are physical concerns that come with overuse of a computer, such as dry eyes, back aches, sleep disturbance, and pain in the fingers and hands.

With all of this potential for problems, it would make sense to teach children about the internet when they are

Children love to play with tablets and phones, but is this a safe practice? Researchers and doctors still aren't 100 percent sure.

older and have the ability to control their use. However, most children are exposed to the internet and internet-based games at very young ages. Advertisers seem to be targeting younger and younger children. Special tablets, cell phones, and even laptops are made with toddlers and pre-kindergarten children in mind. Some schools are even putting technology in their pre-K and kindergarten classrooms. Little research has been done when it comes to the effects of the internet and screen time on very young children. The American Academy of Pediatrics (AAP) recommends that children younger than eighteen months have no time with screens. The AAP also suggests that children five years and younger should have less than one hour of screen time per day. That single hour should be programs that they watch with their parents. Is this what TV in most homes looks like? Maybe not. Marketers don't always design products, like apps, with our health in mind. In the future, we may see more children who are addicted to the internet. Time will tell.

Access

Over the last thirty years, the number of people using the internet has grown, first slowly, then extremely fast. As more countries got online, the number ballooned. Today, about half of the world's population is estimated to use the internet. You might think that the number is spread out over the entire Earth, but in fact, it is quite uneven.

Internet usage is much higher in developed countries such as the United States, the United Kingdom, Japan, and Norway. Some countries, like Iceland, Norway, and Denmark, are nearing 100 percent internet usage within their borders. Other countries, including Liberia, Niger, and Madagascar, have less than 10 percent. According to the Measuring the Information Society Report, richer countries tend to use the internet more than developing nations.

DID YOU KNOW:

North Korea has some of the world's most extreme internet restrictions. The state-controlled network is only available to some university students, researchers, and elite politicians. It is completely closed to outside influence.

In the United States, about 75 percent of the population uses the internet. Similar to the global situation, internet in the United States can be more difficult to access in rural, lower-income areas. While some companies offer lower-cost plans for students, seniors, and lower-income families, these are not offered everywhere, and they do not help fill in all the gaps. The internet is not accessible to all.

When it comes to usage, the problem many have faced is lack of device on which to access the internet. In richer countries, more people have access to PCs, laptops, tablets, and smartphones. In poorer countries, those devices are harder to purchase. However, as technology has become cheaper to produce, more people are able to access the internet through mobile phones. In those countries with low usage, people are acquiring mobile

Internet cafés remain popular in countries and cities where people have limited access to the internet inside their homes and through mobile devices. This is a café in China.

devices quickly. Fewer are purchasing home computers, and fewer are signing up for internet service that connects to their homes. A data plan for a cell phone can be much more affordable.

There is also a gender gap when it comes to internet usage. In wealthier countries, the proportion of women using the internet is about 12 percent lower than the proportion of men. In developing countries, the gap widens to about 30 percent.

Accessibility is a challenge when it comes to those with special needs too. Over the years, new technology has been developed to help people with special sight and sound abilities. There are screen readers that translate words on a screen into recorded speech. There are also braille displays that construct braille characters based on the screen contents. Many websites even include image tags on their website photos so that the screen readers and braille readers can read out a written description of an image. This way, those who are blind can feel as though they are truly "seeing" the website. Along with women and low-income families, people with special needs deserve access to the internet.

Until the issues of accessibility are addressed, the world will continue to be lopsided in terms of who uses the internet. This means that the voices and ideas expressed on the internet are not truly representing our global community. Today, we have the opportunity to push for access, giving all people a chance to participate.

"Smart" thermostats are part of the internet of things. This one tells you the date, weather, and average energy usage.

CHAPTER FOUR

The Internet Today and Tomorrow

When Tim Berners-Lee and researchers at the US Department of Defense were working on the earliest stages of internet networking, they most likely didn't imagine that their invention would gain worldwide use and popularity on today's scale. What started out as a tool for national defense turned into a nearly limitless land of communication, information, and entertainment. We've come a long way from the first room-sized computers, and even from personal computers. Today, the internet is everywhere—in our pockets, in our cars, and even on our wrists. Without it, the world would look much different and, one could argue, it would be a much smaller and less advanced place.

Mobile Technology

When the internet first grew popular with the American public, it was accessed primarily through personal computers, as well as computers located in schools and libraries. These were large machines that sat on desks. In the 1990s, internet networks were connected to the phone line installed in a house or school. Individuals had to "dial in" to access the internet. When you were online, the home phone had a "busy" signal. That meant the house could either be online or on the phone—not both! This wasn't very convenient. Quickly, companies developed technology to get computers connected separate from the phone lines. Today, internet is wireless. The use of routers brings internet into the home and allows multiple computers and devices to be connected at once. Computers can easily connect to a Wi-Fi network, whether you're at home, in a coffee shop, or at a sports stadium. It seems like Wi-Fi is everywhere!

One of the latest technologies that has greatly expanded the internet is mobile data. At first, cell phones were built for one purpose—talking. As technology has improved, people are able to do much more on their phones. They can play games, send email, and stream live videos. They can also communicate using devices other than cell phones. All devices can get online through Wi-Fi networks, but users can also enter internet networks provided by their cell phone carriers. These mobile data networks allow people to access the internet pretty much wherever they are—in the middle of a park, desert, or high on a mountain top.

Many businesses offer free Wi-Fi in order to attract customers. This can be especially helpful for tourists who may not have cell phone data plans that work overseas.

As long as people are paying for data through their cell phone or tablet, they don't need to connect to Wi-Fi to get online. This is revolutionizing the way people use the internet. They can now share live videos, shop, email, use maps, and do so much more, and from nearly any location. This has made the internet more accessible, especially in countries and communities where people do not own laptops or personal computers. Getting online through a cell phone is a more convenient option for people in developing countries, and can be a huge help in moments of emergency, such as when a person is lost and needs to use GPS or find information online.

"Smart" Cars and Homes

Today we live in a truly connected world. In developed countries, the internet is beginning to creep its way into nearly every aspect of our lives. Start-up companies are developing all kinds of new devices that keep us connected all day long. This is commonly called "the

A family living in a "smart" home may be able to control their thermostat, lights, music, security, energy use, and more—all through an app or website.

internet of things." Some of the newest vehicles have internet connections, and many built in the last ten years allow drivers and riders to connect their cars to their phones via Bluetooth technology, which sends a signal from the phone to the car. This way, someone can stream music, listen to podcasts, or talk on the phone through their car speakers.

It seems like the internet is always around. In the twenty-first century, it's certainly appeared in many different, and unexpected, places. In fact, some people now live in houses that are mini-networks of their own. Things like the temperature, lights, security systems, and appliances can be connected to the internet, making them easy to control remotely. A person sitting at work could turn down the home thermostat, lower the lights in different rooms, and check in on a webcam that's pointed at their dog—all with the help of the internet. "Personal assistant" speakers are becoming more popular purchases for a person's home. These are like search engines (Google, Bing) that listen to a person's voice and answer questions. They can be connected to the house, so when someone

STORING YOUR PREFERENCES

Do you ever wonder how Target or the grocery store gives you coupons that seem personally tailored to the products you like? Sometimes, stores seem to know what you want before you even want it. These days, retailers are able to track our shopping habits with ease, all thanks to the internet. Spending habits can be tracked using store loyalty cards, your email address, and phone number. A new technology called geofencing connects to your phone via Wi-Fi or Bluetooth, so stores can detect you when you enter and browse around. Through store apps, you can get specific offers as you wander a store. This could be a little fun … or a little scary! If nothing else, they offer more opportunities for you to get hooked on an item and, ultimately, spend more time and money inside the store.

asks the speaker to do something like "turn the oven to 350 degrees," or "purchase more socks from my favorite website," the action will happen without even the touch of a button. A human voice is all that is really needed when completing tasks in today's most advanced "smart" homes.

All of these tools can make our lives easier and more convenient, but it also means we are never *not* connected. For some, this way of life sounds even more stressful and anxiety-producing than it would be otherwise. It is up to every individual to decide just how "connected" they'd like their life to be. This is a decision that more and more people will have to make as we move forward in our ever-connected and technologically advanced world.

Advertising

All of this internet connectivity is also changing the ways in which people make decisions about what to purchase. A person's decisions are purely their own, right? Not exactly. People can be heavily influenced by advertising. Before the internet, ads were commercials on TV and the radio. You would see ads in print magazines and newspapers too. Today, people still see ads as murals, on the sides of buses and buildings, or in newspapers and magazines. But the internet has taken advertising to an entirely new level. When a person scrolls through websites or apps, they will see some ads that are very clear. They show a product and include words about that product, suggesting the person should check it out and buy it. In the early years of internet ads, these could be banners and buttons that promoted all kinds of products—candy, toys, clothing, movies. Today, most people experience a new kind of targeted advertising. This is done using cookies, or tiny pieces of code that are linked to all of the websites we visit and apps we use. A smart device collects cookies, which can be sold to advertisers.

What do these cookies mean to the average person? It means that when someone looks at a pair of Nikes online one night, they will probably scroll through several Nike and sneaker adds the next morning when they're checking Instagram. If they click on an ad for a hotel, they will probably see many more ads for hotels and vacation products when they use the internet and apps over the next several days. Advertisers are smart. They want to give us the ads we want to see, to influence us to buy. Some people think this is a little creepy—the internet is always watching. Others prefer to see ads for things that they like. It will be interesting to see the new tactics that advertisers come up with as our world continues to connect to the internet in new and different ways.

Health Care

Unsurprisingly, mobile data isn't limited to screens anymore. One of the fastest-growing connected technologies is the world of "wearables." This includes any type of smart electronic device that can be worn on the body. Many of these connect to the internet via Bluetooth or through a wire. Activity trackers are some of the most popular wearables. You can buy all sorts of armbands, necklaces, shoes, and other devices that track your pulse, heart rate, quality of sleep, steps walked, and

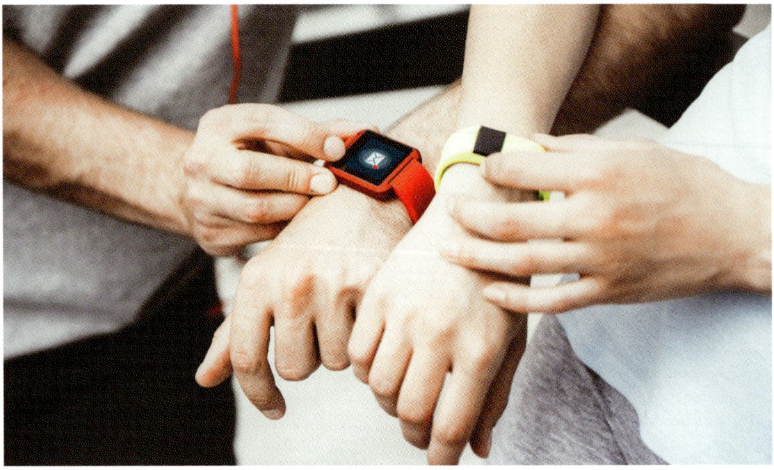

Wearable technology makes the internet even more accessible, and even fashionable.

more. Later, you can track this information through a digital, online display. These devices have been a huge "step" forward for public health. More people every day are logging in to track their personal health and fitness data. They can set goals, compete with friends, and track weight loss, all online, based on real-time data.

While the internet has multiplied the ways that people can engage with their personal health, it has also changed the face of health care as we know it. Today, the health-care industry is turning to technology in order to help the general public improve their health. In its most basic form, the internet allows doctors to connect with resources, as well as other doctors and health professionals, in order to give the best diagnoses and treatment plans.

Taken a step further, the internet has allowed researchers, doctors, and hospitals to utilize the "internet of things" in order to provide better, smarter health care.

Remote monitoring of blood pressure, heart rate, sleep, and perspiration is now possible, allowing health professionals to get fast, frequent updates on their patients' well-being. There are "smart" beds that can detect the presence of a patient, and "smart" homes that can provide all-around care and monitoring to senior citizens.

One of the biggest impacts that the internet has had on the health-care world is through the organization and accessibility of data. Digital, shareable records benefit not only the maze of departments and offices within hospitals, but they allow patients to stay up-to-date on their personal health histories, and help staff know the facts in real time when patients are transferred to their hospitals. Drug companies, insurance companies, doctors, and patients all benefit from the new ease of data storage and sharing. The internet even benefits the receptionists and administrators who deal with appointments—patients are now able to make and cancel appointments online, and reminders can

DID YOU KNOW:

While the internet provides many positive uses for data storage and sharing, it also makes our personal information very vulnerable. Data can be stolen and held for ransom. It can also be shared or destroyed. In 2017, there were more than 2.5 billion data "breaches." A breach happens when vulnerable data is transmitted or copied. Data companies are still figuring out the best ways to protect people's personal information.

Today's "paperwork" is more like screen work! The internet has revolutionized the way we fill out forms, access information, and complete all sorts of business tasks. For some, this is helpful. For those who aren't comfortable with the internet, it can be a challenge.

be sent automatically through email or text. Additionally, the internet provides an entire world of information from which everyday people can learn about their symptoms and sicknesses, helping them to gauge just how necessary that doctor visit or procedure might be.

Without the internet, our day-to-day lives would look completely different. The worlds of business, health care, school, banking, travel, and more have been forever changed. In many ways, the internet has made life easier and better. In other ways, it has created challenges. There's no going back; the internet is here to stay. Those who are growing up today have the opportunity to shape what the internet will look like in the future. How will it help us? How will it hurt us? With the internet, the possibilities are endless.

GLOSSARY

accessibility The design of services or environments that make them able to be reached, used, or appreciated by all people.

ARPANET Also known as the Advanced Research Projects Agency Network, this project was the first internet network to implement TCP/IP.

Bluetooth Technology that enables short-range wireless connection between devices.

cookies Small pieces of data sent from a webserver and stored in a user's computer while browsing a website. These are shared between the website, browser, and server.

cyberbullying Intimidating or threatening behavior that takes place over digital services like social media, websites, text, and apps.

cybersecurity Techniques used to protect against unauthorized use of electronic data.

data Pieces of information, facts, or statistics.

e-commerce Business transactions that occur over the internet.

ENIAC One of the earliest digital, general-purpose computers ever designed and constructed.

geofencing The use of GPS to create a virtual perimeter in a real location, triggering an action when a mobile device enters the space.

hacking Using a computer to secretly gain access to a system, often in order to steal information or cause damage.

hashtag A word or phrase proceeded by a hash sign.

HTML A standard digital language used for creating web pages and web applications.

internet of things Everyday objects that are able to send and receive data through an internet connection.

IP address A unique label made of numbers and periods that is assigned to any device connected to a network. The label shows the computer's location.

network A group of computers or devices that are connected together in order to share resources and exchange data. The internet is an example of a network.

packet switching A type of network in which data, broken down into small blocks (or packets), is moved through the network by a series of devices. These devices identify the packets by unique addresses attached to each one.

PC A personal computer, designed for individual use.

router A tech device that forwards data packets along computer networks.

smartphone A mobile phone that has additional functions such as internet access, email, downloadable applications, and a touchscreen.

social media Websites, social networks, applications, and other types of communication that allow users to create online communities, share content, and send personal messages.

software Various types of programs used by a computer in order to operate.

TCP/IP A set of rules and procedures specifying how data is sent and received over the internet.

telegraph A process for transmitting messages across a distance using a device consisting of one sending instrument and one receiving instrument connected by wire.

trolling Making online posts with the goal of upsetting people or making them angry by posting upsetting, offensive, or inflammatory content.

URL A uniform resource locator, this is the address of a webpage on the World Wide Web.

wearable Technology that can be worn on the body or as part of one's wardrobe.

World Wide Web A space on the internet that can be accessed using a browser, which allows user to search for information, shift between pages, and connect documents to one another.

FURTHER INFORMATION

Books

Bruzzone, Catherine. *STEM Starters for Kids Technology Activity Book.* New York: Skyhorse Publishing, 2017.

Portersfield, Jason. *Tim Berners-Lee.* Tech Pioneers. New York: Rosen Publishing, 2016.

Saujani, Reshma. *Girls Who Code: Learn to Code and Change the World.* New York: Viking Press, 2017.

Smibert, Angie. *The Internet.* How It Works. Mendota Heights, MN: North Star Editions, 2017.

Wallark, Laurie. *Grace Hopper: Queen of Computer Code.* New York: Sterling Publishing, 2017.

Websites

Code Monster

http://www.crunchzilla.com/code-monster

This coding game is extremely easy to use, and it's a ton of fun!

NoBullying.com

https://nobullying.com

Check out this site for information on cyberbullying, statistics, and ways to get help.

Videos

Coding: By a Kid, for Kids TEDxKentState

https://www.youtube.com/watch?v=vOsdfRbrNdk

Eleven-year-old Krish Mehra has already created two published apps. Here, he gives a TED Talk about learning to code.

History of the Internet

https://www.youtube.com/watch?v=Dxcc6ycZ73M

This video is the introduction to the series "How the Internet Works." It gives a brief overview of internet history. The series is produced especially for young people.

How Does Wi-Fi Work?

https://www.youtube.com/watch?v=co4rLn9N8OU

This fun video uses drawings to demonstrate how Wi-Fi works.

What Is the Difference Between Cellular and Wi-Fi Data?

https://www.youtube.com/watch?v=-bSiNVUCLG0

Watch this video to learn the difference between cellular and Wi-Fi data, two different ways to access the internet on phones and mobile devices.

SELECTED BIBLIOGRAPHY

American Academy of Pediatrics. "American Academy of Pediatrics Announces New Recommendations for Children's Media Use." AAP.org. October 21, 2016. https://www.aap.org/en-us/about-the-aap/aap-press-room/pages/american-academy-of-pediatrics-announces-new-recommendations-for-childrens-media-use.aspx.

Cameron, Darla. "How Targeted Advertising Works." *The Washington Post*. August 22, 2013. https://www.washingtonpost.com/apps/g/page/business/how-targeted-advertising-works/412.

Copeland, Jack B. "The Modern History of Computing." *Stanford Encyclopedia of Philosophy*. 2006. https://plato.stanford.edu/entries/computing-history.

Hafner, Katie. *Where Wizards Stay Up Late: The Origins of the Internet*. New York: Simon and Schuster, 1998.

International Telecommunications Union. *Measuring the Information Society Report 2017: Volume 1*. 2017. https://www.itu.int/en/ITU-D/Statistics/Pages/publications/mis2017.aspx.

Kamenetz, Anya. "Screen Addiction Among Teens: Is There Such a Thing?" NPR. February 5, 2018. https://www.npr.org/sections/ed/2018/02/05/579554273/screen-addiction-among-teens-is-there-such-a-thing.

Lafrance, Adrienne. "The Internet in Space? Slow as Dial-Up." *Atlantic*. June 11, 2015. https://www.theatlantic.com/technology/archive/2015/06/the-internet-in-space-slow-dial-up-lasers-satellites/395618.

Levine, Yasha. *Surveillance Valley: The Secret Military History of the Internet*. New York: PublicAffairs, 2018.

Michael, Paul. "8 Ways Retailers Are Tracking Your Every Move." *Time*. September 25, 2016. http://time.com/money/4506297/how-retailers-track-you.

Poppy, Carrie. "New System Could Give 16 Million People With Special Needs Internet Access." *Tech Times*. October 27, 2015. http://www.techtimes.com/articles/100335/20151027/new-system-give-16-million-people-special-needs-internet-access.htm.

Ramsey, Lydia. "How the Internet Is Improving Health Care." *Business Insider*. https://www.weforum.org/agenda/2017/01/technology-is-changing-the-way-we-view-our-health-this-is-how.

Ryan, Johnny. *A History of the Internet and the Digital Future*. Islington, UK: Reaktion Books, 2013.

Williams, Martyn. "How the Internet Works in North Korea." Slate. November 28, 2016. http://www.slate.com/articles/technology/future_tense/2016/11/how_the_internet_works_in_north_korea.html.

INDEX

Page numbers in **boldface** are illustrations.

accessibility, 6–7, 15–16, 21, 24–25, 27, 36, 41–43, 46–47, 53
addiction, 39, 41
Amish, 10, **11**
ARPANET, 16–19, **17**

Berners-Lee, Tim, 21, 23, **23**, 27, 45
Bluetooth, 48, 49, 51
browser, **12**, 21–22, 23, 25

calculator, 14
Cerf, Vincent, 19
challenges, 20, 22, 27, 29, 43, 54
circuit switching, 16–17
commercial use, 18, 20, 24–25, 27, 30, 32
communication, 8, 9, 10, 13–14, 16–17, 22, 24–25, 29, 32, 45–46
cookies, 51
cyberbullying, 34
cybersecurity, 36

data, 8, 16–17, 19, 22, 27, 36, 52–53
definition, 24–25
Department of Defense (US), 16, 18–19, 22, 24, 29, 45
dot-com companies, 24–26

e-commerce, 30–32
email, 5, 8, 9, 10, 18, 22, 26, 32, 46–47, 49, 54
ENIAC, 14, **15**

Federal Networking Council (FNC), 24

Gamergate, 34
geofencing, 49
governance, 22, 27
GPS, 6, 11, 47

hacking, 35–36
hashtag, 37

health care, 51–54
HTML, 23

infrastructure, 20, 24
internet movements, 37
internet of things, 48, 52
invention, 5, 13–15, 23
IP address, 22

Kahn, Robert E., 19

Licklider, Joseph Carl Robnett, 16

Main Street, 31
mobile data, 39, 43, 46–47, 51

National Science Foundation (NSF), 25
Netscape, **12**, 21
network, 16–21, 35–36, 41, 45–46, 48
nodes, 18

packet switching, 17
PC, 14–15, 25, 42, 45–47

postal service, 10, 13
privacy, 33–34, 36

research, 7, 16, 19–22, 24, 40
router, 46

safety, 35, 37
screen time, 40
smartphone, 5, 26, **27**, 42
social media, 6, 9, 13, 33, 37, 39
software, 15, 35

targeted advertisements, 40, 49, 51
TCP/IP, 19, 24
telegraph, 10, 14
trolling, 34

URL, 23

wearable, 51, **52**
Wi-Fi, 6–7, 46–47, 49
World Wide Web, 10, 21, 23, 27

ABOUT THE AUTHOR

Kaitlyn Duling believes in the power of words to change hearts, minds, and, ultimately, actions. An avid reader and writer who grew up in Illinois, she now resides in Pittsburgh, Pennsylvania. She knows that knowledge of the past is the key to our future and wants to make sure that all children and families have access to high-quality information. She has written over forty books for young readers. The internet is one of her favorite places to be.